Alex Bogdanov

Jokes all the way from Russia for British people to enjoy. 18+!

Copyright © Alex Bogdanov (2021)

The right of Alex Bogdanov to be identified as author of this work has been asserted by him in accordance with section 77 and 78 of the Copyright, Designs and Patents Act 1988.

Any person who commits any unauthorised act in relation to this publication may be liable to criminal prosecution and civil claims for damages.

WARNING!

A number of jokes in this book are strictly 18+. If you are not a fan of swearing, adult content or sexual innuendos this book is not for you.

ACKNOWLEDGEMENTS

I would like to thank my wife Sara Bogdanov and my friend Stephanie Hayden for their help in my project. It wouldn't be accomplished without their support.

PREFACE

Thank you for buying this book. I have lived in the UK for more than ten years. Do you know that there are no quality books about Russian humour in the English language? Not even online. The majority of the books are either full of boring, silly jokes or full of old Russian jokes. Some jokes in those books are translated literary without any cultural differences taken into consideration, so only a Russian person will understand them. No wonder my British friends think that there is no humour in "Mother Russia".

Well it is your lucky day. I have gone through thousands of Russian jokes and funny stories to find the top ones and that are understandable for British people. I have translated the jokes taking into consideration the modern English language. Sadly, not every joke can be translated. There are so many good jokes in Britain and in Russia. But as soon as you translate them from English into Russian or vice versa the jokes lose their meaning and are no longer funny.

Don't forget you can purchase this book in an audio version. So you can listen to the jokes if you don't like to read. The audio version has my voice so you can enjoy hearing the jokes in a Russian accent.

Remember this book has adult jokes that you might find too sexual, offensive or rude. In this book you wont find childish jokes, knock knock jokes or one-liners. Not every joke in this book is rude or contains foul language, but still I would like to warn you. The book is split into to four chapters – Softcore, Hardcore, HardcoreXL and Unusual jokes. Softcore has no swear words. Hardcore has some and HardcoreXL has plenty. The last chapter has a few jokes only. They deserve to be in this book, but how funny they are will depend on your taste.

When you will be in Russia or in a country where Russian language is spoken don't forget to tell them some of these jokes I promise Russian speaking people will understand them.

Alex Bogdanov, or Alexey Bogdanov, Aleksejs Bogdanovs or Алексей Богданов basically suit yourself.

Wales, Llantarnam.

01.06.2021

CONTENTS

Chapter One
Softcore Jokes
Nr 1 – Nr 52

Chapter Two
Hardcore Jokes
Nr 53 – Nr 82

Chapter Three
HardcoreXL Jokes
Nr 83 – Nr 113

Chapter Four
Unusual Jokes
Nr 114 – Nr 121

CHAPTER ONE

Softcore jokes

Nr 1

Bum

A wife came home from a doctor's appointment and said to her husband, 'Doctor told me that he never saw a 50-year-old woman like me. He said that my breasts look like a 20-year-old breasts.'

Husband asked, 'Did he say anything about the saggy 50-year-old bum?'

'Oh, no darling, he didn't mention you at all.'

Nr 2

Unknown location

One guy took to many drugs and woke up in an unknown location with a police officer standing above him. The guy was lying on the ground, looking around. It seemed he was in a big city. 'Where am I?' he asked.

'Don't you see the Kremlin? You are lying in the Red

Square,' replied the police.

The guy got irritated. 'The hell with the details! What city? Name the city?'

Nr 3

Dumb

Husband came back home and found his wife with a lover. 'What is happening here?' he shouted.

The wife looked at the lover with a sad face, 'I told you he is dumb, bless him.'

Nr 4

British tourist

A British tourist hired a car and was travelling in Russia. One day she was stopped by the police and was told that she was speeding.

'It's not true I didn't,' she said in broken Russian giving the ticket back.

The police replied, 'Fine, here is a pen and paper. Please write down your explanation and you can go without the fine.'

'But I barely speak Russian. I can't write,' she replied.

'We don't care. Sit here until you will finish writing.'

She sat for half an hour and didn't write anything. After not knowing what to do she decided to put a

£50 note on top of the papers and give them back. When police took the papers they noticed the £50 note and said, 'And you told us that you can't write. I can see that half of the explanation is already written.'

Nr 5

Alcohol debate

Animals were debating which animal has the best anatomy for drinking alcohol. The hippo said, 'I do. Because I have the biggest mouth, I take the biggest mouthful and taste the drink properly.'

The elephant said, 'No, I do. I can drink with my trunk and the sensation is unbelievable.'

The giraffe said, 'No, I do. I have the longest neck. You can't even imagine how nice it feels when the drink is slowly flowing and flowing down my neck.'

Hippo laughed, 'Is that so? And if you vomit? He-he.'

Nr 6

Donations

Three religious leaders met and discussed how they distribute the donations. One leader said, 'We do it simply. We draw a circle on the floor and toss the donations into the air. What falls in the circle goes towards godly deeds, the rest we take for ourselves.'

The second leader said, 'We do it similarly. Only instead of a circle, we draw a line. Everything that falls on the right side is for God, everything that falls on the left side is for us.'

The third leader said, 'We have a much easier way. We put more trust in God then you do. We throw the donations in the air. Everything that God wants God will take. Everything that is left is ours.'

Nr 7

Hangover

A bear woke up with a hangover. He crawled to the nearst lake to have water and to get better. As the bear was drinking a hunter came out of the bushes and shot at the bear. The bear didn't react and continued to drink. The hunter approached the bear pushed the gun into the bear's body and shot again, but the bear didn't react. After a moment the bear looked up and sighed, "What the hell was in that vodka yesterday? I supposed to feel better after drinking water, but every second I feel worse and worse."

Nr 8

Bull

A child was running through a field. He was late for lunch. The mother was screaming, 'Where have you been? You left your phone in the house!'

The child replied, 'Everything is fine mum. Grandad asked me to take our cow to see the bull. So, I did.'

His mother asked, 'Your grandfather couldn't do it himself?'

The child got confused. 'I think he could, but mum I think the cow prefers the bull.'

Nr 9

Gravedigger

New guy was put in a prison. All the inmates were keen to find out what he was in for. He said, 'All my life I was a gravedigger and sometimes I would open coffins. Nothing ever happened, but this time I was in for a surprise.'

'Go on,' said everyone.

'A few months ago there was a gangster's funeral. His family decided to bury him with all of his golden rings. When I saw them, I was like that's it this is my chance. I can't miss it. So, one week after the funeral I decided to dig up the grave. As soon as I opened the coffin and touched one of the rings this guy woke up, shoved some documents in my face and shouted, 'Inspection! Trading Standards!'

Nr 10

Big man

When a husband came home his wife was in the bedroom. The husband suspected there is a lover in the house. He heard somebody in the bathroom. He rushed there and found a huge, 7-foot-tall bloke taking a shower.

The bloke turned off the shower and said, 'Well that's it you found me.'

The husband quickly replied, 'No, no I still need to look in the kitchen and I missed the garage.'

Nr 11

Soft drink

A beer convention has ended. Different beer representatives went to a local pub to have a drink. Budgeysir representative ordered a pint of Budgeysir, Hanakan representative ordered a pint of Hanakan, Pepponi representative ordered a pint of Pepponi and so on. Only Guinness representative ordered a soft drink.

All of the representatives got puzzled and asked, 'Why did you order a soft drink?'

Guinness representative replied, 'Out of solidarity. You didn't order beer, so I didn't.'

Nr 12

Happiness

'How is Boris? I heard Olga left him.'

'He is much better now. But in the beginning we were really worried about him. He nearly died from happiness.'

Nr 13

Lucky

One woman on the way to work bought a lottery ticket and won £100 000. When she came to work, she found that her arsehole manager was fired. "What an amazing day, it's like winning lottery twice," thought the woman.

When she came home her husband opened the door full of tears and said, 'My mother passed away.'

The woman jumped in the air and shouted, 'Woohoo Hat-Trick!'

Nr 14

True love

Wife is angry. 'You are such a bad husband! You only think about yourself. You are so selfish!'

The husband replied, 'I am selfish? I only think about myself? Do you know that I love your mother in law more than I love my mother in law!'

Nr 15

Fishmonger

A husband was drinking with his friends, but he told his wife he went fishing. On the way home, he stoped at a fishmongers to buy a live fish. 'Can I have three of those please?'

'Yes, sure,' said the fishmonger.

The husband asked, 'I have just one small request. Can you please throw it over the counter, and I will catch it?'

'Why would you want to do that?'

'So I can say with a clear heart to my wife that I caught the fish.'

Nr 16

Three doctors

After work a dentist, a pathologist and a gynaecologist were walking home. The dentist said with happiness, 'Finally we are outside. Fresh air, fresh air! I am so tired of human breath.'

The pathologist added, 'Yes, and everyone is alive around us. Everyone is alive.'

The gynaecologist said, 'Yes, and faces. Finally, I am looking at faces!'

Nr 17

Clothes

Potheads were in a flat. There was a knock on the door. They slowly came to the door and opened it. It was the police. 'What is going on here? Your neighbours complain that they can hear horrible laughter and a smell of burnt clothing! What are you doing here?'

Potheads replied confused, 'What do you mean "what are we doing"? We are burning clothes, laughing.'

Nr 18

Weed

One pothead bought herself some super quality weed. She sat down by the window, made herself comfortable and started to smoke. No effect. She took another drag. Still no effect. "They sold me some crap," she thought. Her grandmother came into the room, placed a hand on the pothead's shoulder and said, 'I know you don't like when I disturb you, but please go and do something. You have been sitting by the window for two weeks now.'

Nr 19

Painting

A group of people were on a tour in a museum in Moscow. They came to a painting by the name "Prince Albert in France". They looked at the painting. It was of a bed with four feet pocking out from under the quilt.

The tour guide said, 'If you will look closely. You will notice that these feet belong to Queen Victoria and those feet belong to John Brown.'

Someone from the group asked, 'John Brown? What about Prince Albert?'

The tour guide pointed at the painting's name and said, 'Prince Albert is in France.'

Nr 20

Brush

A guy was sitting in a kitchen and eating as his mother in law came in with a sweeping brush. The guy asked her, 'Dear mother in law, are you planning to clean here? Or are you finally flying away?'

Nr 21

Hop

'Waiter? Waiter?' asked a customer.

'Yes?' came the waiter.

'Do you have frog legs?'

'Yes.'

'Righto, hop along and bring me your best wine.'

Nr 22

Cliff

Two climbers are climbing a tall, steep mountain. Suddenly one of the climbers lost their grip and fell down into the mist. The other climber was looking down trying to see anything, 'Are you OK? I can't see you!'

The falling climber shouted, 'I am okeeeyyy, I am still faaalliiing!'

Nr 23

Funeral

At a pothead's funeral, all of the friends came high. Pothead's mother was standing by the coffin and cried, 'Why? Why did you take those drugs? Now you will go to a place with no family, where you won't have a warm bed, where you will be cold, where no one will make you dinner, where you won't be loved!'

One of the potheads looked at everyone scared and said, 'Hey this is not funny. When did you arrange to carry him to my place?'

Nr 24

Sparrow

A husband came back from a long business trip and found his wife in the arms of another man. The wife said to the husband, 'Oh, you are my poor sparrow. While you were flying around an eagle landed in this house and made a nest.'

Nr 25

Auction

In Moscow at an auction designated for oligarchs, a couple bought a painting for £50 million. The wife looked at the husband and said, 'Well I am happy with this birthday card. Let's go and look for the present.'

Nr 26

Desert

A woman was walking through a desert. At one point she couldn't walk anymore, she fell and landed by a genie lamp. Excited she got up and rubbed it. A genie appeared and said, 'You have three wishes.'

The woman was shocked. 'Is it true? You can grant wishes?'

'Yes,' the genie said.

'I want to go home.' Genie took her by the hand and started walking with her. 'No, no,' the woman said, 'I want to be home faster.' The genie started to run.

Nr 27

Abortion

In a University a student had a test. The professor asked him, 'Can you do an abortion on a cow?'

The student didn't know what to answer and asked. 'I am very sorry professor; I really need to use the toilet. Can I?'

'OK, fine,' said the professor.

The student ran out of the class and tried to find an answer online but the signal was blocked. The student ran around trying to find someone, but the hall was empty. The student ran into the toilet and stumbled upon potheads. 'Guys can you do an abortion on a cow?'

Potheads looked shocked. 'What a real cow?'

'Yes,' the student said.

'Whoa, mate?! You got yourself into a real mess, didn't you?!'

Nr 28

Branch

A climber lost his grip and began to fall. He managed to grab hold of a branch that was sticking out of the cliff. With all his strength he was trying to hold on. 'God! God! Please save me!' he was screaming.

The sky became clear and a roaring sound came down. 'My son, do you truly believe in me?'

'Yes, I do,' shouted the climber.

'Let go of the branch and I will save you,' said God.

The climber replied. 'Right, you have had your say. Is there another God?!'

Nr 29

One vs All

A woman was arguing with all of the church. 'I am right. You all are wrong. I am the only one correct.'

The church replied, 'We don't care. You are alone in your views. We all think you are wrong.'

'I will prove to you I am right.' She raised her hands and shouted, 'God, please tell them that you are on my side.'

A thunderous voice came down from the sky, 'My daughter I am on your side!'

'You see even God is on my side,' said the woman.

The members of the church smirked and said, 'So? It's you two against all of us.'

Nr 30

Prophet

People were throwing stones at a person. A prophet

came out of the crowd and stopped everyone. 'I will only allow you to throw a stone if you yourself are without a sin!' The crowd moved back, but an old lady jumped out of the crowd, threw a stone and killed the person. The prophet said angry, 'Mother how many times I've told you don't interfere with my business!'

Nr 31

Atheist

In a University a professor wanted everyone to understand that God doesn't exist, so the professor said, 'Students, don't be afraid of god. God doesn't exist. Let's open a window and spit at god. You will see that nothing will happen.' One by one students came to the window and spat. Only one girl did not participate. The professor asked her, 'Why are you not spitting? Are you afraid of god?' All the class laughed.

The girl replied, 'Well firstly if God doesn't exist you all look like complete morons spitting out the window for no reason. And secondly, if God does exist why the hell do I need problems?'

Nr 32

Catholic school

While a Jewish family was living in Israel their son

had very bad marks in school. But when the family moved to Europe and sent their son to a catholic school he became the top student and they only heard good reports from his teachers.

One day they decided to find out what happened. 'David, our beloved son. We spoke to your teachers and they said that from day one you were the best student. They were shocked to find out that you had problems in your previous school. What happened David?'

David replied, 'I wanted to tell you this, but I was afraid. On my first day I found myself in one of the halls. There I saw our fellow Jew, tortured, and hanged on a cross. Straight away I realised this school doesn't tolerate bad behaviour.'

Nr 33

The greatest showman

An announcement in a circus. 'Attention! Our next performance will be carried out by our gymnasts.'

A male voice came from the crowd, 'All gymnasts are morons!'

Next announcement. 'Attention! Our next performance will be carried out by our clowns.'

Again, the same male's voice came from the crowd, 'All clowns are morons!'

Next announcement. 'Attention! Our next performance will be carried out by our fire breathers.'

Again, same voice. 'All fire breathers are morons!'

Next announcement. 'Attention! A performance never seen before. A jump from 60 feet without any safety ropes!'

Same voice in the crowd. 'Where are you dragging me, you morons?'

Nr 34

Art of jokes

A young man was imprisoned for the first time. He was sitting with mature prisoners and was trying to understand a strange game they were playing. One prisoner said "42" and everyone laughed. The other prisoner said "9" and everyone laughed. Then someone said "121" and everyone laughed. The young man interrupted them. 'I don't want to disturb you, but what is this game you are playing?'

'It's not a game boy,' said one prisoner. 'It is jokes. We have been sitting together for such a long time that we know all of our jokes through and through. So instead of repeating them, we assigned a number to every joke.'

'Can I try?' asked the boy.

'Sure.'

The young boy thought for a second and said, '87.'

Old prisoners looked at each other unimpressed and continued to tell numbers to each other and laugh.

The young boy was offended. 'What happened? What did I do wrong? No one even smiled?'

The old prisoner said, 'You didn't do anything wrong son. You are just crap at telling jokes.'

Nr 35

Idiot

A husband is arguing with his wife. He said to her, 'You are stupid, you are an idiot!'

The wife replied, 'Well if I would have married a smart man I would have been smart.'

Nr 36

Poor and Greedy

A poor person knocked on a greedy person's door. The greedy person opened the door and asked, 'Yes, what do you want?'

The poor person replied, 'I am hungry, I have not seen food for days!'

The greedy person shouted into the house, 'Olga? Olga? Can you please show this poor man a burger?'

Nr 37

Scottish pub

A few Scottish friends were sitting in a pub slowly sipping whisky. They have noticed that at a nearby table a man was drinking whisky pint after a pint.

'Look at him, what is he doing? Go and explain to him the right way to drink whiskey,' said one friend to another friend.

'OK, I will.' After a few minutes, he came back.

'So? What's wrong with him?' asked his friends.

'Oh, don't worry about him he is not Scottish he is Russian.'

Nr 38

Tea or Coffee

'Waiter I can't understand is this tea or is it coffee?'

'Well, how can I help you if you cant taste the difference between tea and coffee!'

Nr 39

Young wife

A friend asked a newly wedded husband, 'So what it's like? Married life?'

'I am very tired,' replied the husband, 'She is constantly going to every pub, to every bar.'

'She has drinking problems?' the friend asked.

'No, no. She is trying to drag me back home.'

Nr 40

Anatomy

Husband and wife were watching an anatomy programme. The husband said, 'It is amazing how they do the operations these days. How easily they can turn a man into a woman and a woman into a man. Have you ever wanted to become a man?'

The wife answered, 'Not really. And you?'

Nr 41

Anaesthetic

'Hi, Boris! How was the operation?'

Boris replied disappointed, 'Argh, it was boring. I was under anaesthetic.'

Nr 42

Parcel

Olga sent Boris a message. 'Boris, I want to terminate our relationship. Please don't text and don't call me. Can you please post all of my belongings that I have left in your house?'

A few weeks passed by. Boris followed the request. He didn't call or text. Eventually, Olga received her parcel. It was full of strange stuff with a note on top. The note said, 'Olga, the 5 years we were dating I had so many women I have no clue what stuff belongs to you. Can you please take what is yours and send the rest back? Boris.'

Nr 43

Law school

A teacher in a law school told one student. 'This work is written in a very complex language. It is very difficult to understand. You have to remember when you will have a job you have to write in a way that even stupid people will understand.'

The student replied, 'OK teacher, what you don't understand?'

Nr 44

Three words

A professor was asking new students, 'What are the three most popular words in our Uni? Anyone? Boris?' Do you know?'

Boris got shy. 'I don't know.'

The professor replied happy, 'Well done, that is the correct answer.'

Nr 45

Canteen

In a canteen, a professor put his food on the table and left to grab a drink. A student came along pushed professor's food out of the way and took the professors seat. The professor came back and said appalled, 'Student! Do you know the difference between humans and animals?'

'Yes, I do. Humans sit while eating and animals stand. Mwah-ha-ha,' student laughed.

Nr 46

Early break

Boss told his employees that he has to leave the office and he won't be back for the rest of the day. After an hour one of the employees said, 'Guys, I am going home. The boss is not coming back.'

The employee entered his house and smelled wine and cigars. He slowly walked through the house and saw his boss and his wife in the bedroom. He quickly rushed back outside and ran to the office. In the office, he jumped behind the computer and started to work. Everyone asked him concerned, 'What happened? What happened?'

The employee replied, 'I think the boss saw me. If he will ask anything say I was here all day.'

Nr 47

Grandfather

A grandchild full of tears rang the other granchild. 'I am so sorry to tell you this. I have bad news about grandfather.'

'Oh, no what happened,' replied the other grandchild.

'Well we were in an orchard and grandfather decided to pick apples by himself, so he climbed all the way up to the top and fell . . . We lost him.'

'Lost him? Is the grass that long?'

Nr 48

Blind

A blind person entered the shop with a guide dog. The blind person tightly got hold of the lead and started to swing around the dog above the head. The manager ran to the blind person and asked, 'Hello! Do you need any help?'

The blind person replied, 'No, thank you. I am just looking around.'

Nr 49

Baptised

An old lady came to a church with a dead dog and asked the priest, 'Excuse me father, can we have a funeral service for my doggy?'

Father got angry. 'What are you talking about! It is a

dog! We don't do services for animals. It is a sin.'

The old lady said, 'But father this doggy is the only friend I had all my life.'

'No, I can't. It is against our believes.'

'But what shall I do father?'

Father waved his hand, 'There are Jehovah's Witnesses down the road ask them.'

The old lady started to walk away, but then turned around and asked, 'Father, I only have £10 000 pounds will that be enough for Jehovah's Witnesses?'

Father rushed towards the old lady and said, 'Sister, sister? Why you didn't tell me that your doggy is a baptised Christian?'

Nr 50

Cold body

A mother in law passed away. At her funeral she was lying in an open coffin. One by one people came to say their goodbyes. Only her son in law stopped and put his head on her chest and didn't move for five minutes.

After the funeral, his mate asked him, 'Why did you do that? Everyone knows you hate your mother in law. Why did you put your head on her chest for so long?'

'You got it all wrong,' replied the son in law. 'I had

so much to drink last night and my head is banging today. But the mother in law she was so lovely and cold.'

Nr 51

Cold morning

Early in the morning husband got up and went fishing. After walking for half an hour, he decided to go back because it was cold, wet and damp. He quietly opened the front door. Gently walked into the bedroom, slowly got back under the quilt and put his arm around his wife.

The wife didn't open her eyes and whispered sleepely. 'You are early today and you are so cold. It must be freezing outside, but as every Tuesday my idiot went fishing.'

Nr 52

Two islands

A plane has crashed in an ocean. One man survived and ended up on an island. He searched the island through and through, but didn't find anyone. For a whole year, he had to survive alone. One day he had enough and decided to swim to a neighbouring island which was miles away. He barely made it to the second island. There he was met by a woman.

'Finally, civilisation!' he shouted.

'No civilisation here,' she said, 'I am alone. I have been alone for many years.'

'Oh, no I came from the other island. I was alone for a whole year too!'

She smiled, 'Don't worry. Come to me. I have something that you have desired for a long time.'

The man shouted, 'No way! You have internet!'

CHAPTER TWO

Hardcore Jokes

Nr 53

A tank of beer

A boss of a brewery rushed to his employee's house. The wife opened the door and the boss said, 'I am so sorry, I have bad news about Boris. He fell into a tank full of beer. He didn't make it.'

Wife started to cry, 'That is awful. I hope he didn't suffer.'

Boss replied, 'I am sure he didn't. He even emerged a few times to take a piss.'

Nr 54

Alcohol test

A police officer stopped a car full of drunken girls. They argued with him that they were not drunk, but he was not having it. 'Out of the car and give me your keys,' he said. But they stayed inside. While he was arguing with them, he noticed that they were looking at his groin area. He got embarrassed and asked,

'Why are you looking down there?'

The girls continued to look at his groin and giggled, 'Officer, get your breathalyzer out, we are ready to blow on it to prove we are not drunk.'

Nr 55

It fits

A husband came back home. He went into the bedroom and saw a massive, 7-foot-tall lover on top of his wife having sex. Husband quickly found his cricket bat, run back into the bedroom and smacked lover's arse. The lover stopped moving, looked at the wife and grinned. 'Huh, and you said it won't fit in.'

Nr 56

Island

A Russian tourist came to Britain and was travelling around. When she got to the seaside, she decided to have a chat with a local old man. 'Hello. I am a tourist. Where will I get if I will take this road?'

'You will end up by the sea,' replied the old man.

'And if I will take that road?'

'Again you will end up by the sea.'

She asked annoyed, 'Wait a second and if I will take that road over there?'

'Child, no matter which road you will take you will

always end up by the sea! Fucking island.'

Nr 57

Russian language

One British person after studying in Russia came back to the UK and said to his friends, 'Russia is a mysterious country and their language doesn't make any sense. Listen to this. "Fence" is pronounced – "Zabor", "Cathedral" is pronounced – "Sabor", and when you can't take a shit it's pronounced – "Zapor". Absolute nightmare!'

Nr 58

Dildo

A father walked in on his daughter masturbating with a dildo. 'Don't worry, don't worry. I am leaving,' he said.

The next day the daughter came home from school and saw something strange. Her father was drunk on the sofa and opposite him was her dildo with a shot glass. 'Dad! What is going on?'

'Everything is fine daughter. I just decided to have a drink with my future son in law.'

Nr 59

Bear hunt

Two friends decided to go on a bear hunt. In the forest unpredictably they stumbled upon a bear. They panicked and started to climb up a tree. The bear followed them. They have reached the top and then one of the friends decided to shoot the bear. He fired once and blew off one of the bear's balls. He shot again and blew off the second ball.

The other friend shouted in panic, 'What the fuck are you doing?! The bear is climbing here to eat us! Not to fuck us!'

Nr 60

Attack

A famous gynaecologist was detained for attacking a woman on the street. A police officer asked him, 'You are a reputable man in this town. Why did you attack that homeless woman?'

'Officer, please try to understand me,' replied the gynaecologist, 'I had a busy day. I was with women all day. I couldn't wait to get back home. I was walking as fast as I can and that woman jumped in front of me and said, "For some money, I can show you my pussy."'

Nr 61

First night

Newlyweds were enjoying their wedding night. Husband asked the wife to swallow. 'I don't want to do it,' she replied.

'Please, it's our first night,' he said.

'No,' wife said.

'Why?'

'First of all, I never did it before and secondly it gives me heartburn.'

Nr 62

Romeo and Juliette

Romeo and Juliette were smoking a joint. Romeo said, 'I have a feeling that I love you, Juliette.'

Juliette replied, 'This weed is weird. I feel the same shit.'

Nr 63

Red dildo

A woman that enjoyed rough sex walked into a sex shop. 'Can I have the black dildo, the yellow one and the red one please?'

The cashier replied puzzled, 'You can buy the black dildo and the yellow dildo. But about the red fire extinguisher, I need to speak with the manager.'

Nr 64

First visit

After her 18th birthday a girl decided to visit a sex shop for the first time. She was looking at different dildos. The cashier gave her some dildos to hold and feel them. The girl was very shy and didn't know which one to buy. She looked around and asked, 'Where are the fitting rooms?'

Nr 65

Millionth wedding

Journalists were standing by the registry office. They were waiting for the millionth couple to marry in this office. When the newlyweds came out the journalists were shocked. They saw a tall, broad woman and tiny, small man. A journalist said to the bride, 'Love works in mysterious ways. Does it?'

The bride replied, 'Love? What love? My mother told me that all man are turds. So, I decided to have the smallest lump.'

Nr 66

Sperm units

Teacher in a University asked the students, 'How much sperm on average does a man ejaculate?'

One girl shouted, 'A lot!'

'I understand, but I need more specific measurements.'

The girl said, 'Three gulps.'

Nr 67

Farm inspection

Owners of a big farm looked at the accounts and something didn't add up. The farm was making less money than it should. The owners spoke to their employees but didn't find anything suspecious. So, they decided to hire an animal whisperer.

The owners and the whisperer went to see the cows. 'Moo-oo,' the cows said.

The whisperer translated, 'The cows said that the cow manager is stealing milk.'

The owners looked at the manager, 'Wait for us in the office.'

Then they went to speak with the pigs. 'Oink, Oink,' the pigs said.

The whisperer translated, 'From every pig that gave birth the manager stole one piglet.'

The owners looked at the manager, 'Wait for us in the office.'

Then they went to speak with the sheep. 'Bah, bah,' the sheep said.

Suddenly the sheep manager jumped in front of the sheep and said, 'Don't listen to those sheep! It only happened once, and I was drunk!'

Nr 68

Tricky question

In a University a philosophy teacher said to a student, 'There is not a lot I can do. You will have a bad mark for this work. But there is a game we can play. Ask me a question, if I will find it interesting and I won't be able to answer it, I will give you the top mark. If I will answer it, I will give you the lowest mark. OK?'

'Hm, risky. But let's play,' said the student. 'Here is the question. What is lawful, but doesn't make sense? Makes sense but is unlawful? And both unlawful and doesn't make sense?'

'That is a very interesting question.' The teacher thought for ten minutes and couldn't answer. So he gave the student the top mark and asked, 'OK, tell me the answer? I am quite intrigued.'

The student inhaled. 'OK, here we go. That such an old man like you has a beautiful young wife is lawful, but doesn't make sense. That your beautiful wife is cheating with a young, handsome lover makes sense, but is unlawful. And that you gave this lover a top mark is both unlawful and doesn't make sense.'

Nr 69

Babushka

One guy was fishing in a forest. He was there all morning but didn't catch any fish. He was sitting on the ground sad. An old babushka came by and asked, 'Why are you sad?'

The man replied, 'I have been fishing all morning, but the bucket is empty.'

'Throw in your fishing rod now,' babushka said.

The man followed her words and straight away caught a big fish. He got scared and asked, 'Old lady are you baba-yaga?'

'Yes, my son. I am,' she said.

'Can you do anything else for me?'

'Sure, no worries,' babushka said.

'Can I have a bigger house?'

'Done. Go home you have a bigger house.'

'I came here in a tiny car. Couldn't even get into the forest. Can you give me a modern 4X4?' asked the man.

'Sure, I can, but only if you can do something for me?' asked babushka.

'Yes, anything,' the man replied.

'I am very old and I haven't had a man for a long time. Will you be able to have sex with me?'

'Easy!' said the man and had sex with babushka.

When everything was done the old lady looked at

him and asked, 'How old are you, young man?'

'I am 37,' he replied.

Babushka smirked and said, 'Not a young boy anymore, but still believe in fairy tales.'

Nr 70

Condoms

A father and his child came into a pharmacy. By the counter, the child noticed that condoms were laid out in a strange way. A row of thee. A row of six and a row of twelve. 'Daddy why are they placed like that,' asked the child.

Dad answered, 'It's done according to age groups. The three condoms are for comp students. Two condoms are used Saturday night and one Sunday morning.'

The child continued. 'And the six condoms?'

'Those are for University students. Two are used Friday night, two are used Saturday night and two Sunday morning.'

'And the twelve condoms?'

Dad replied, 'Those are for married couples. One is used in January. One is used in February . . .

Nr 71

Monkey

On a beach, a person was standing with a monkey. Someone came up and asked, 'How much does it cost? With the monkey?'

The person replied hesitantly, 'Um, do you mean to take a photo?'

Nr 72

Jealous friend

In a small village, in a local club everyone was dancing, except two girls. They were trying to find a partner to dance with, but everyone was taken. Suddenly a big man came in and approached the girls, he grabbed one of them and they started dance. Her friend felt jealous because she was left alone. When the girl that was dancing went to the toilet the big man sat next to the girl that was jealous.

'I have never seen you here before,' she said, 'Are you from another valley?'

'No, I from here,' he replied.

'But I never seen you?' she said.

'I was in prison for a long time. Only got out yesterday,' he said.

'Why were you in prison?'

'I killed my partner.'

When the girl came back from the toilet she asked her jealous friend, 'Did you have a chat with him?

What do you think of him?

The jealous friend replied, 'You are very lucky. I found out that he is single.'

Nr 73

Stranger

In a big mansion, a little girl ran into the bathroom and shouted, 'Mummy, mummy there is a stranger in the spare room having sex with our maid!'

Mother jumped out of the bath all wet. 'Quickly call the police!'

The little girl started to laugh, 'April fools mummy, the stranger is our daddy.'

Nr 74

New car

One guy is grilling his friend, 'How come you still don't have a car? Come on buy a car? We can go for a ride in your new car. We can have so much fun.'

The other friend replied, 'Listen stop pestering me everyday. I don't speak to you like that. I don't tell you "Come one find a girlfriend. Why are you still single. Go and get a girlfriend! We can have so much sex together!"'

Nr 75

Deep

'Hello!' shouted gynaecologist.

'HELLO, Hello, hello.' it echoed.

Nr 76

Time

A voice on a radio. 'Moscow time is twenty hundred hours (20.00). For those who doesn't understand it is 8.00 pm. For the stupid ones - the small hand points at 8 and the long hand points at 12. And for absolute idiots, the small hand points at boobies.'

Nr 77

Recycling

A wife has asked her husband. 'Darling, can you please sort out the recycling and take it outside?'

Husband was staring at the telly and said, 'It is not a husband's duty to do recycling.'

Wife got angry, took off her robe, got naked, lied on the sofa, spread her legs, and said, 'Fine, do your husband duties!'

The husband looked at her, stood up and sighed, 'Right, where is that recycling.'

Nr 78

New employee

A female boss hired one of her male friends. On the first day at work, this male employee put his head under her skirt. 'This is harassment! Have you lost your marbles?' she shouted and pushed him away.

The employee replied confused, 'But. But you said yourself if I want to have a career in your company I have to start at the bottom?!'

Nr 79

Lottery

A man ran into his boss's office. He smacked his boss on the head, climbed on top of the table, kicked everything around, pulled his penis out and started to wee. One of the other employees slowly opened the door and quietly said, 'Boris, there was a mistake. You didn't win the million quid. Sorry.'

Nr 80

Living room

Two neighbours had a chat on the street, 'I am very sorry neighbour, but I have to tell you this. Yesterday I was passing by your house and in the living room window, I saw you and your Mrs running around naked. It was so funny. I laughed so much. You both naked! I laughed all night.'

Neighbour replied, 'Well prepare yourself, you will

laugh even more, I wasn't home yesterday at all.'

Nr 81

Proper job

A husband found his wife with a lover. He didn't react, he only closed the door and walked away. His wife jumped out of the bed, opened the bedroom door and shouted, 'Oh no you don't, come back and watch how its properly done!'

Nr 82

Marriage duties

A wife stumbled upon her husband having sex with a lover. She didn't get angry; she told them to get dressed and leave the house.

The wife was standing outside having a fag. The lover came to her and said, 'I am so sorry. I didn't know he was married.'

The wife replied to her, 'I just don't understand why did you sleep with him? I have marriage duties, but who forced you?'

CHAPTER THREE

HardcoreXL Jokes

Nr 83

Swallow

Two high class escorts got together and started to discuss their earnings for the month.

The first escort asked, 'How much did you earn?'

'I made £10 000. And you?' the second escort replied.

'How is that? We worked the same hours, but I only made £9 000!'

'Hm, that is strange. Did you swallow by any chance?'

'Yes, I did. Why?'

'Well, it all makes sense then. They have deducted meal money.'

Nr 84

Fishing

A young boy decided to take up fishing. At the lake the fish wasn't biting. A few hours passed by, but still nothing. An old man came, started fishing and after an hour left with a bucket full of fish. The young boy rushed to him and asked, 'What bait do you use?'

'Maggots,' replied the old man.

'Ah, I had worms my fault.'

The next day the young boy used maggots, but still no result. Again the old man came and after an hour left with a full bucket. The young boy caught up with him and asked, 'I used maggots, but it didn't help.'

'I didn't use maggots today. I used worms.'

'So how do you know when to use maggots and when to use worms?'

'It is easy. When I wake up, I lift my quilt. If my penis is on the left side, I use maggots. If it is on the right side, I use worms.'

The young boy got shy. 'And if it is ... erected . . . hard?'

The old man said, 'Huh, if the penis is hard why the fuck do you need fishing?!'

Nr 85

Sherlock and Watson

Watson asked Sherlock, 'How come man's pubic hair is rough and wiry, and woman's pubic hair is soft and gentle?'

Sherlock replied disturbed, 'Watson, stop asking silly questions. Keep on sucking.'

Nr 86

Let it go

A young boy and a young girl met at a club. After dancing all night, they decided to leave together. They came to her gate and stood awkwardly for a few minutes. "Well it's about time we do something," the boy thought. He took out his penis and put it in her hand.

The girl screamed, 'I thought you were going to kiss me, but you did this vile thing. Pervert!' She opened the gate and ran to her front door. While she was trying to open the door, she could feel a heavy breath down her neck. She turned around and saw the boy. 'No-o, what do you want? Leave me alone you pervert!'

The boy replied calmly, 'You idiot, I would have left already. Let go of my dick!'

Nr 87

Worst wedding

A guest at a wedding got very drunk and wondered from table to table. The drunk guest finally sat down at one of the tables and spoke, 'This is the worst wedding ever. Boring as fuck. The groom looks ugly. The bride looks ugly–

The drunk guest got interrupted, 'Are you not embarrassed? How dare you? How dare you say such horrible things about my daughter!'

The drunk guest replied, 'Oh, I am so sorry. If only I knew that you are the bride's father, I would never say such a thing.'

'That's it. Now you have really fucked up. I am her mother!'

Nr 88

Blow

At a wedding groom's friend got very drunk and when people were giving speeches he stoond up and said, 'I wish that the bride give me a blowjob.'

The groom rapidly got up in anger. 'What did you say?'

The drunk friend looked at the groom, 'I understand you probably want to do it as well. But tonight, I specifically want the bride to do the blowjob.'

Nr 89

Geography

Supply geography teacher started to work in a new school. As soon as she entered the classroom the whole class shouted, 'Piss off!'

Without saying a word, the supply teacher burst into tears and ran to the headmistress. The headmistress siad, 'Don't tell me. Its Year 7? SW?'

'Yes,' she cried.

'Oh, those... Again! OK, follow me.' The headmistress grabbed a globe and took the teacher back to the classroom. The headmistress kicked the classroom door open. 'Good morning you little shits. How are you today?'

Children replied scared, 'Hello, headmistress.'

'Say "Hello" to your new teacher,' said the headmistress.

All children said, 'Hello, teacher.'

The headmistress put the globe on the table and asked, 'Right, do any of you know how to put a condom on a globe?'

'What is a globe?' children asked.

'That will be explained to you by your new geography teacher.'

Nr 90

Bushes

Two potheads came to a brothel. At the front door, the mistress of the place told them that the starting price is £300.

'Uh, we only have £50,' the potheads said.

Mistress laughed, 'Well for £50 you can go and fuck

yourselves in those bushes.' She closed the door.

After half an hour there was a knock on the front door. The mistress opened it and saw the same potheads.

'Thank you,' said the potheads and passed over £50.

Nr 91

Shakes

Three alcoholics were talking. 'That's it I have to stop drinking. I can't live like this anymore. I can't text anything, my fingers keep shaking,' said one.

The second one said, 'Yes, I will stop as well. My hands are shaking so much that when I try to have a drink, I spill everything.'

The third one said, 'I have to stop too. My hands are shaking terribly. Every time I try to take a piss I cum myself.'

Nr 92

Dress

In a dirty nightclub a man and a woman were having sex in a toilet cubicle. The man was having her from behind and the woman kept trying to grab the man and scratch him. The man asked irritated, 'Stop moving I am trying to hold you. What is wrong with you?'

The woman moaned, 'The dress . . . The dress is

caught on your penis.'

Nr 93

Three men

In a nightclub a woman went into the toilets and found three men having sex. She ran to the bar. 'Barmen! Barmen! There are three guys having sex in the laddie's toilet.'

Barmen asked, 'Was there a green-haired man?'

'Yes, the other two were fucking him! I can't believe it.'

The barmen sighed jealously. 'I can't believe it either, he always gets lucky,'

Nr 94

Horny boy

In a school, an excited boy came to a female teacher and said, 'I want to have sex with you.'

The teacher replied, 'How dare you? You cant say that to me. I am your teacher!'

'That's absolutely fine. You can teach me while we do it.'

Nr 95

Horny boy 2

Another day and the excited boy asked the female teacher, 'I want to have sex with you.'

'Right I had enough,' she replied, 'I know I am a teacher, but do you know that I actually hate children!'

'Not a problem, I brought condoms.'

Nr 96

Pirates

Pirates hijacked a cruise ship. They split the men and the women into two groups. 'Right all women please jump overboard, and we will watch how sharks will tear you apart. Men, you will become our concubines.'

Women complained. 'This is ludicrous? "Men-concubines"! Where did you even see such a thing!'

Men replied, 'Whoa, whoa, watch your mouth! Of course, men can be concubines. Go and jump to those sharks!'

Nr 97

Johnny

In a small town Novgorod, scientist Boris was trying to create a robot that was very good at sex. He nearly finished the project but had to go away on a business trip. Before going to the airport, he said to his wife,

'Olga, if you want you can test my robot. When you are ready just shout "Johnny, fuck" and the robot will have sex with you.'

'OK, Boris. We will see,' said Olga.

A few hours passed by and Olga decided to do it. 'Johnny, fuck!' she said. Johnny jumped at her and was having her for a few hours. When Olga had enough, she realised that Boris didn't tell her how to turn off the robot. She tried everything to stop Johnny, but Johnny didn't stop.

"Luckily we live in a semi house," thought Olga and started to knock on the wall. 'Katya! Katya!' Her neighbour Katya ran into the house. 'I can't stop it, I can't stop it,' screamed Olga. 'Can you please take over? Just shout "Johnny, fuck!"

Katya said, 'OK, I will help you.' She shouted "Johnny, fuck!" and the robot jumped on her. Olga tried to phone Boris, but he didn't pick up. So she rang her friends to come over and help. More and more people came over. They smashed the robot; they shot at the robot, but nothing helped. The only thing they could do is to shout "Johnny, fuck" and take it in turns.

Boris landed somewhere in Asia and remembered that he didn't tell Olga how to turn off Johnny. He phoned her but she didn't pick up. He phoned friends and neighbours, but no body was picking up the phone. He took the next plane back to Russia. When he landed in Moscow he jumped in a taxi. 'Please, take me to Novgorod!'

The taxi driver looked at him petrified. 'Novgorod! No-o, I am not driving there. Didn't you hear about Johnny?'

Nr 98

Fall

A roofer was working on a block of flats and fell. As he was falling an arm reached out from a window and caught him. The roofer heard a voice. 'If you will give me a blowjob, I will save you.'

'No way,' the roofer replied, and the arm let go of him.

He continued to fall. Another arm reached out, caught him and the roofer heard another voice. 'If you will lick my pussy, I will save you.'

'No-o,' shouted the roofer and the arm let him go.

He continued to fall until another arm caught him. The roofer shouted, 'I will lick you; I will suck you. Please save me!'

A different voice from the window said, 'For fuck sakes. What a generation of people. I am looking for someone to have a drink with. But people only think about fucking.' The person let go of the roofer.

Nr 99

Curtains

Two friends were talking. 'Listen, Olga, I have a problem?'

'What's wrong?' asked Olga.

'The party went well yesterday, but when all of you left something strange happened.'

'What?'

'Nothing major I am just asking everyone. Do you know the difference between toilet paper and curtains?'

'No,' said Olga.

The friend replied, 'Oh, you dirty cunt. So, it was you!'

Nr 100

Old man

Somewhere in a village three friends were having a drink in a local pub. At some point, an old man came to one of them and said, 'I fucked your mum.' The three friends tried not to react, and the old man left.

After a while he came back and said to the second friend, 'I fucked your mum.' Again, the friends decided not to do anything, and the old man left.

But later the old man came back and said to the third friend, 'I fucked your mum.'

All of the three friends stood up and said to the old man, 'Dad, when you are pissed can you please stay home!'

Nr 101

Pinocchio

Pinocchio became a teenager and decided to have a go at wanking and set himself on fire for fuck's sake!

Nr 102

Pinocchio 2

Pinocchio fell in love. He asked Geppetto to make him a penis. When the work was done. Pinocchio with happiness ran back to his girlfriend. Later that day Pinocchio and his girlfriend came back to Geppetto. 'What have you done Geppetto?' asked the girl, 'I can't have sex with Pinocchio I will have splinters inside.'

'Not, a problem,' said Geppetto. He grabbed a sandpaper and rubbed Pinocchio's penis until it was smooth. 'There you go.'

The girl said satisfied, 'Let's go Pinocchio.'

Pinocchio looked at Geppetto and said quietly, 'Who needs girls! Geppetto pass me that sandpaper?'

Nr 103

Maniac

One night three friends left a pub drunk. On the way

home, they were captured by a serial killer that cut of penises. The maniac said to them, 'The rules are as such. If the combined length of your dicks is 36 inches I will let you go. If it will be less, I will chop them off.'

The first guy measured his penis – it was 18 inches. The second guy measured his penis – it was 15 inches. The third guy measured his penis – it was 3 inches.

The maniac unhappy said, '36 all together. Hum, I have to let you go.'

The three friends were walking home and the first one said, 'What would you do without mine 18 inches?'

The second guy said, 'What would you do without mine 15 inches?'

The third guy said grumpy, '18 inches, 15 inches... Be grateful that I made myself excited.'

Nr 104

Psychologist

A man came to Moscow to seek help, 'Doctor, you have to help me. I am always depressed, and nothing helps me?'

'Did you try tablets?' asked the doctor.

'Yes, no effect.'

'Did you try some strong alcohol?'

'Yes, no effect.'

'Did you try to spend more time with women?'

'Yes, I did. Nothing helps I am always sad,' the man replied.

'OK, maybe you need to try to sleep with men?'

'I did that too it doesn't help.'

'Did you try drugs? Weed?'

'Yes, doctor I did. Nothing helps me, I am always depressed.'

'Well, I can only advise you to go to Siberia. There is a clown Boris and he does miracles. He can make anyone happy.'

'So much for your fucking help doctor! I am that "Boris" the clown!' Shouted the man and jumped out of the window.

Nr 105

Parent's house

A teenage couple was sitting home with parents. They were talking about cats, school, viral videos and so on. When the parents left, the young couple could finally stop talking about crap and enjoy a good fuck.

Nr 106

Mirror

A man had a bath. When he came out, he started to look at himself in the mirror. He had a look at his left side and at his right side. When he turned around and saw his arse, he felt how his penis got erected. He grabbed his penis and said, 'Calm down its only me.'

Nr 107

Married life

Newlywed couple Boris and Olga were having a conversation. Boris said, 'That's it from now on as soon as I come home, we have sex. I don't care if you are tired or not and I don't care if you have a headache or not.'

Olga replied, 'Fine, but I have one request as well.'

'Go on,' said Boris.

'From now on every Wednesday at 7 pm at our house there will be a wild orgy and I don't care if you are present, or not.'

Nr 108

Positions

Parents left their child in a sitting room to do homework and went upstairs to have sex. The child got fed up of homework and went up to find parents. The child came to the bedroom door and through a small gap was watching parents having sex in different positions. The child said in disgust, 'Eww, and they tell me I can not to pick my nose! Disgusting.'

Nr 109

Slut

A teacher, a father and his daughter had a meeting. The teacher in tears said, 'Your daughter called me a slut!'

Father yanked his daughter by the sleeve and said, 'How dare you say things like that! She is your teacher; she looks after you! It is none of your fucking business what she does after work!'

Nr 110

A lot of sex

A woman asked her doctor, 'Doctor you have to help me. I like clubbing and I like to have sex. I like to have a lot of sex. Every week I go out clubbing and have sex with a stranger, but when I wake up in the morning I always feel like a total idiot. Can you help me?'

The doctor thought and said, 'I can give you these tablets they will reduce your sex drive and eventually you will be able to say no to sex.'

'Whoa! Hold on doctor. I am keeping the sex. Can we do something about me feeling like a idiot after?'

Nr 111

Football coach

A football coach went to check if his team were asleep and found everyone awake. In anger, he shouted, 'Half an hour ago I told you "Good night". Fuck! When I say, "Good night" I am saying "Shut your fucking eyes and go to sleep, you idiots"'

The team replied, 'Yes, sir. Good night, sir.'

Nr 112

Boris

Boris passed away. Pathologists were working with his body. One of them said, 'Look at his penis have you ever seen a penis this size?'

The other pathologists replied, 'No, never. It is huge.'

'We will have to keep it a secret. I will remove the penis and take it home to study.' The pathologist cut the penis off, put it into a glass jar, poured preservatives over it and placed it into his rucksack.

When he came home his wife met him at the door. 'Come on, faster, you are always late, the food is getting cold.' She took his coat and the rucksack as he went to the bathroom.

In the bathroom, the pathologist heard how his wife was screaming. He thought, "On no, I forgot about the jar."

As he was running to the kitchen, he could hear his wife screaming, 'Oh no! Oh, no! Boris is dead!'

Nr 113

Sailor

A ship came to the dock after a long journey. A sailor ran off the boat, as quickly as he could, back home to have sex with his wife. As they started to have sex she realised he slid into her bum. 'Why didn't you tell me you wanted anal. I didn't wash. I am not ready!' she said.

The sailor replied, 'Fuck the destination I need to unload my ship asap.'

CHAPTER FOUR

Unusual Jokes

Nr 114

For the lovers of cartoon humour

Dark web

Timon and Pumbaa became very poor. Someone told them that there are many ways to become rich on the dark web. They decided to check it out. One-night Timon scrolled through different ads and found someone who was looking for animals to make clothing out of.

The next day Timon took a knife and went to Pumbaa's place.

Timon said, 'I didn't find anything on the Dark Web. Did you?'

'Yeah, nothing interesting,' said Pumbaa.

Simultaneously Timon and Pumbaa jumped and both pointed knives at each other.

'Liar and you call yourself a friend,' said Pumbaa.

'Shut up you fucking jacket!' said Timon.

'You shut up, you fucking fur coat!' said Pumbaa.

Nr 115

For the lovers of art humour

Filmmakers

At a celebrity gathering, two filmmakers have met for the first time. 'Very nice to meet you,' one said, 'What do you film?'

'I mainly film about love,' the other filmmaker replied.

'Oh, about the love between two males?'

'No.'

'About love between two females?'

'No.'

'I know, between a mother in law and a son in law?'

'No, just the typical love between a man and a woman.'

The other filmmaker lost enthusiasm and said, 'Uh, you like to film safely. No wonder I don't know your work.'

Nr 116

For the lovers of economical humour

Japan

JOKES ALL THE WAY FROM RUSSIA FOR BRITISH PEOPLE TO...

A Japanese factory worker came at 8 am and left at 11 am. After leaving early for a couple of days the rest of the employees got fed up with him. The next time he finished working early all of the employees surrounded him. 'Where to hell do you think you are going so early?' They came closer ready to punch him.

The factory worker shouted, 'Mates what are you doing? I am on a two-week holiday!'

Nr 117

For the lovers of philosophical humour

Basic terms

In University a Philosophy teacher asked her new class to explain in basic words what is the difference between common-sense, dialectic and philosophy. Everyone was using smart words. The teacher was not happy. She wanted someone to explain it simply, but no one could.

'OK, class I will help you. Imagine two people are walking on the street. One is dirty and one is clean. Which one is going to the bathhouse?'

'The clean one,' some students said.

'No, the clean one is clean. There is no need for him to go to the bathhouse. The dirty one must become clean. So, the dirty one is going. That is called common sense. OK, again. Two people are walking. One is dirty and one is clean. Which one is going to the bathhouse?'

'The dirty one,' students said.

'No, the dirty one doesn't wash; hence he is dirty. The clean one is going to the bathhouse hence he is clean all the time. Now, this is called dialectic. OK, again two people are walking. One is dirty and one is clean. Which one is going to the bathhouse?'

One of the student's whispered, 'Who the fuck knows?!'

The teacher looked at the student and said, 'Exactly! Now that students is called philosophy.'

Nr 118

For the lovers of political humour

Crisis

Russia is in crisis. The elite got together to find a new leader. They decided it would be, Olga. They arranged for her to speak in front of the people outside Kremlin.

At the meeting, Olga shouted to the masses, 'If you will elect me. I will make sure that instead of 5 days a week you will be working 4 days a week!'

'Yeah!' the crowd shouted

Olga continued, 'If I will stay in power for 10 years, you will be working 3 days a week!'

'Yay!' the crowd cheered.

'If I will stay in power for 20 years, you will be working 2 days a week!'

'Hooray,' the crowd supported the idea.

After the meeting, Olga met with the elite. They asked her, 'So how did it go? What is the future of our country?'

'The future looks grim. I had a chat with the nation and realised that the nation has no fucking desire to work.'

Nr 119

For the lovers of silly humour

Indecisive

Journalists are speaking to the Russia's most indecisive person. 'So, tell us please what's it like to live without knowing what you want.'

The person replied, 'Horrible, absolutely horrible. For example, I love tea with sugar. But even that is a big problem for me. When my friends offer me a cup of tea, I ask for three sugars. When I make a cup of tea for myself, I put one sugar. But I think I like two sugars.'

Nr 120

For the lovers of Shakespeare humour

Brutus

In Moscow, an amateur theatre is trying to become famous by setting William Shakespeare's play Julius Caesar with a twist.

Act 3. Curtains opened. An actor was standing in the centre of the stage and said, 'I am Caesar!'

The second actor came out with a knife. 'I am Brutus.'

The third actor came out with a knife. 'I am Brutus.'

The fourth actor came out with a knife. 'I am Brutus.'

Caesar looked at the fourth one. 'And you Brutus?'

Nr 121

For the lovers of dark humour

Ashes

After the funeral a wife came home with her husband's ashes. She opened the lid of a sand timer and replaced the sand with his ashes. She put the timer in the kitchen and said, 'You bastard! You thought you could escape so easily. You will continue to work for me.'

JOKES ALL THE WAY FROM RUSSIA FOR BRITISH PEOPLE TO...

I hope you had a good laugh,

The End

Facebook - @alexbogdanovuk

Instagram - @alexbogdanovuk

ALEX BOGDANOV

Twitter - @alexbogdanovuk

Printed in Great Britain
by Amazon